CAMBRIDGE
Wit & Humour

CAMILLA ZAJAC

BRADWELL
BOOKS

Published by Bradwell Books

9 Orgreave Close Sheffield S13 9NP

Email: books@bradwellbooks.co.uk

Complied by Camilla Zajac

British Library Cataloguing in Publication Data: a catalogue record for
this book is available
from the British Library.

1st Edition

ISBN: 9781902674933

Print: Gomer Press, Llandysul, Ceredigion SA44 4JL

Design by: jenksdesign@yahoo.co.uk

Illustrations: ©Tim O'Brien 2013

Two Cambridge University students were in the middle of an argument when their lecturer came into the room.

The lecturer asked them, "Why are you arguing?"

One student replied, "We found a ten pound note and decided to give it to whoever tells the biggest lie."

"You should be ashamed of yourselves," said the lecturer, "When I was your age I didn't even know what a lie was."

The students gave the ten pound note to the lecturer.

How many Oxford University academics does it take to change a light bulb?

None. That's what research students are for.

You can have me but cannot hold me;
Gain me and quickly lose me.
If treated with care I can be great.
And if betrayed I will break.
What am I?

Trust.

Harry proudly drove his new convertible into town and parked it on the main street, he was on his way to the Charity Shop to get rid of an unwanted gift, a foot spa, which he left on the back seat.

He had walked half way down the street when he realised that he had left the top down... with the foot spa in the back.

He ran all the way back to his car, but it was too late...
Another five foot spas had been dumped in the car.

What kind of coat can only be put on when wet?

A coat of paint.

A man from Oxford went into a hardware store and asked to buy a sink.

"Would you like one with a plug?" asked the assistant.

"Don't tell me they've gone electric!" said the man.

I am seen in places that appear to need me not.
I come seldom to places that need me most.
Sometimes my arrival is celebrated,
at others times I am hated.
I refresh all things whether they need it or not.

Rain.

Did you hear about the two men from the monastery who opened up a seafood restaurant? One was the fish friar, and the other was the chip monk.

A farmer from Chipping Norton once visited a farmer from Wisbech. The Chipping Norton farmer asked "How big is your farm?" to which the Wisbech farmer replied "Can you see those trees over there? That's the boundary of my farmland".

The Chipping Norton man responded, "Wow. It takes me three days to drive to the boundary of my farm."

The Wisbech man said "I had a car like that once."

What has a head like a cat, feet like a cat, a tail like a cat, but isn't a cat?

A kitten.

A man from Chesterton wanted to become a monk so he went to the monastery and talked to the head monk.

The head monk said, "You must take a vow of silence and can only say two words every three years."

The man agreed and after the first three years, the head monk came to him and said, "What are your two words?"

"Food cold!" the man replied.
Three more years went by and the head monk came to him and said "What are your two words?"

"Robe dirty!" the man exclaimed.
Three more years went by and the head monk came to him and said, "What are your two words?"

"I quit!" said the man.
"Well", the head monk replied, "I'm not surprised. You've done nothing but complain ever since you got here!"

The leader of a vegetarian society just couldn't control himself any more. He just needed to try some pork, just to see what it tasted like. So one summer day he told his members he was going away for a break. He left town and headed to the nearest restaurant. After sitting down, he ordered a roasted pig, and impatiently waited for his delicacy. After just a few minutes, he heard someone call his name, and to his horror he saw one of his fellow members walking towards him. Just at that same moment, the waiter walked over, with a huge platter, holding a full roasted pig with an apple in its mouth. 'Isn't that something,' says the man after only a moment's pause, 'All I do is order an apple, and look what it comes with!'

What was given to you, belongs to you exclusively and yet is used more by your friends than by yourself?

Your name.

A gloomy looking man was sitting in a cafe in Huntingdon. He picked up the menu and noticed that it only featured three dishes: meatloaf, shepherd's pie and Yorkshire pudding. The waitress came over to take his order. "I'll have the Yorkshire pudding," said the man glumly, "and if you could throw in a few kind words that would be very welcome." The waitress left and returned a few minutes later with a plate of Yorkshire pudding. She banged the plate on the table in front of the man and started to walk off. "Hey," said the man. "I got my dinner; how about those kind words?" The waitress turned, paused and said, "Don't eat the Yorkshire pudding."

A girl who was just learning to drive went down a one-way street in the wrong direction, but didn't break the law. How come?

She was walking.

A man from Cambridge phoned his son in Oxford three days before Christmas and said, "I hate to ruin your day but I have to tell you that your mother and I are divorcing; forty-five years of misery is enough."

"Dad, what are you talking about?" his son shouted.

"We can't stand the sight of each other any longer" his father said, 'We're sick of each other and I'm sick of talking about this, so you call your sister in London and tell her."

Frantic, the son called his sister, who yelled "Like hell they're getting divorced!" she shouted, "I'll take care of this!".

She immediately called her father and yelled at him 'You are not getting divorced. Don't do a single thing until I get there. I'm calling my brother back, and we'll both be there tomorrow. Until then, don't do a thing, DO YOU HEAR ME?''. Then she hung up.

The old man hung up his phone and turned to his wife. "Sorted! They're coming for Christmas - and they're paying their own way."

A man is rushing to a hospital from a business trip because his wife has just gone into labour with twins, and there is a family tradition that the first family member to arrive gets to name the children. The man is afraid his wayward brother will show up first and give his kids horrible names. When he finally arrives at the hospital in a cold sweat he sees his brother sitting in the waiting room, waving, with a silly grin on his face. He walks unhappily in to see his wife who is scowling and holding two little babies, a boy and a girl. Almost afraid to hear it, the man asks, 'What did he name the girl?' 'Denise' says the wife. 'Hey that's not too bad! What did he name the boy?' 'De-nephew.'

What has five eyes, but cannot see?

The Mississippi River.

At a well established manufacturing business in Chatteris, the young boss had the sad responsibility of telling one of the workers, Joe, that it was time for him to retire after 60 years with the company.

The old man was outraged:

"So, it's come to this, has it? I'm not wanted any longer?" he protested. "I worked for your father, your grandfather and his dad too.

I tell you what, young man, if I'd known that this job wasn't going to be permanent, I would never have taken it on."

A man builds a house rectangular in shape. All the sides have southern exposure. A big bear walks by. What colour is the bear? Why?

The bear is white because the house is built on the North Pole.

Two men were waiting to be served in a Cambridge butcher's shop. One of them said "I bet you £100 that you can't reach that piece of meat on the ceiling and the other man said "I'm not betting!". The first man said "Why not?" and the other man said "The steaks are too high!".

What can you catch but not throw?

A cold.

I have holes in my top and bottom, my left and right and in the middle. What am I?

A sponge.

A Ramsey school pupil asked his teacher, "Are 'trousers' singular or plural?"

The teacher replied, "They're singular on top and plural on the bottom."

If vegetarians eat vegetables, what do humanitarians eat?

I never was, am always to be,
No one ever saw me, nor ever will,
And yet I am the confidence of all
To live and breathe on this terrestrial ball.
What am I?

Tomorrow.

They say that a man from Oxford laughs three times at a joke: the first time when everybody gets it, the second a week later when he thinks he gets it, the third time a month later when somebody explains it to him.

The outcome of the annual Oxbridge Boat race is very predictable. It's always Oxford or Cambridge.

I'm part of the bird that's not in the sky. I can swim in the ocean and yet remain dry. What am I?

A shadow.

Did you hear about the Oxfordshire lorry driver who was seen desperately chiselling away at the brickwork after his lorry got stuck while passing through a tunnel?

'Why don't you let some air out of your tyres?' asked a friendly passer-by.

'No mate,' replied the man 'It's the roof that won't go under, not the wheels'.

Stan and Alf worked at a sawmill in Whittlesey. Alf was known for being very accident prone. One day, he slipped and his arm got caught and severed by the saw. Stan quickly put the arm in a plastic bag and rushed it and Alf to the local hospital. Next day, Stan went to the hospital to ask about Alf. The nurse said, "Oh he's fine, we've reattached his arm". Alf was back and hard at work at the sawmill the very next day.

However, within a couple of days, Alf had another accident and severed his head. Stan put the head in a plastic bag and rushed it and Alf to the hospital. The next day he went in and asked the nurse how Alf was. The nurse broke down and cried and said, "He's dead". Stan was shocked, but not surprised, and said to the nurse: "I suppose the saw finally did him in".

"No", said the nurse, "Some idiot put his head in a plastic bag and he suffocated".

A Teversham man once bought two horses, but soon realised that he couldn't tell them apart. So he asked the farmer who lived next door what he should do. The farmer suggested measuring them.

The man came back triumphantly and said: "The white horse is two inches taller than the black horse!"

A duck walks into a pub and goes up to the barman.

The barman says 'What can I get you?'

Duck: 'Umm. Do you have any grapes?'

Barman (Looking surprised):

'No, I'm afraid we don't.'

The duck waddles slowly out of the pub.

The next day at the same time, the duck waddles into the pub, hops up on a bar stool.

Barman: 'Hi. What can I get for you?'

Duck: 'Um. Do you have any grapes?'

Barman (a little annoyed): 'Hey! Weren't you in here yesterday. Look mate, we don't have any grapes. OK?'

The duck hops off the stool and waddles out of the door.

The next day, at the same time, the barman is cleaning some glasses when he hears a familiar voice

Duck: 'Umm.. Do you have any grapes?'

The barman is really annoyed

Barman: 'Look. What's your problem? You came in here yesterday asking for grapes, I told you, we don't have any grapes! Next time I see your little ducktail waddle in here I'm going to nail those little webbed feet of yours to the floor. GOT me pal?'

So the duck hops off the bar stool and waddles out.

The next day at the same time, the duck waddles into the pub, walks up to the barman and the barman says,

'What on earth do YOU want?'

'Errrr. do you have any nails?'

'What!? Of course not.'

'Oh. Well, do you have any grapes?'

What goes around the world but stays in a corner?

A stamp.

At an antiques auction in Cambridge, a wealthy American announced that he had lost his wallet containing £5,000, and he would give a reward of £50 to the person who found it. From the back of the hall a local man shouted, "I'll give £100!"

What gear were you in at the moment of the impact?
Gucci sweats and Reeboks.

What gets wetter and wetter the more it dries?

A towel.

An American photographer on holiday was inside a church in Garsington, taking photographs when he noticed a golden telephone mounted on the wall with a sign that read '£10,000 per call'.

The American, being intrigued, asked a priest who was strolling by what the telephone was used for.

The priest replied that it was a direct line to heaven and that for £10,000 you can talk to God.

The American thanked the priest and went along his way.
Next stop was in Witney.

There, at a very large church, he saw the same golden telephone with the same sign under it.

He wondered if this was the same kind of telephone he had seen in Garsington and he asked a nearby nun what its purpose was.

She told him that it was a direct line to heaven and that for £10,000 he could talk to God.

"OK, thank you," said the American.

He then travelled to Bicester, Cowley, Wantage, Didcot and Thame.

In every church along the way, he saw the same golden telephone with the same '£10,000 per call' sign under it.

The American continued his grand tour to Cambridgeshire.

He arrived in March, and again, in the first church he entered, there was the same golden telephone, but this time the sign under it read '50 pence per call.'

The American was surprised so he asked the priest about the sign. "Father, I've travelled all over Oxfordshire and I've seen this same golden telephone in many churches. I'm told that it is a direct line to heaven, but in Oxfordshire the price was £10,000 per call. Why is it so cheap here?" The priest smiled and answered, "You're in Cambridgeshire now, son...it's a local call."

All about, but cannot be seen.
Can be captured, cannot be held.
No throat, but can be heard.
What is it?

The wind.

A passenger in a taxi tapped the driver on the shoulder to ask him something.

The driver screamed, lost control of the cab, nearly hit a bus, drove up over the curb and stopped just inches from a large plate glass window.

For a few moments everything was silent in the cab, then the driver said, 'Please, don't ever do that again. You scared the daylights out of me.'

The passenger, who was also frightened, apologised and said he didn't realize that a tap on the shoulder could frighten him so much, to which the driver replied, 'I'm sorry, it's really not your fault at all. Today is my first day driving a cab. I've been driving a hearse for the last 25 years.'

Local Police hunting the 'Knitting Needle Nutter' who has stabbed six people in Histon in the last 48 hours, believe the attacker could be following some kind of pattern.

After an inter-university boat race, the mother of one of the losing Oxford crew consoled her son.

"Never mind dear," she told him," You were wonderful. You rowed faster than anyone else in your boat."

When one does not know what it is, then it is something; but when one knows what it is, then it is nothing?

A riddle.

A boy from Littleport was getting ready to start his new school term. Because he was getting older and more independent, his father gave him £2 for him to catch the bus home. But instead of getting on the bus, the boy ran behind it all the way home. His father came home and the boy proudly said, "Dad, I saved you £2 today because I ran behind the bus instead of getting on!" The man stormed out of the room, shouting "You should have run behind a taxi and saved me 40 quid you little..."

What comes once in a minute, twice in a moment, but never in a thousand years?

The letter M.

A new client had just come in to see a famous lawyer.

'Can you tell me how much you charge?', said the client.

'Of course', the lawyer replied, 'I charge £200 to answer three questions!'
'Well that's a bit steep, isn't it?'

'Yes it is,' said the lawyer, 'And what's your third question?'

What goes round the house and in the house but never touches the house?

The sun.

Two blokes went into the Plough in Great Shelford.

The first man said "A pint o' bitter, and a half o' shandy for my mate 'Donkey', please!"

The publican replied "'What's with him calling you 'Donkey'?"
The second one said "Oh, 'e aw, 'e aw, 'e always calls me that!"

You can have me but cannot hold me;
Gain me and quickly lose me.
If treated with care I can be great,
And if betrayed I will break.
What am I?

Trust.

A group of chess enthusiasts checked into a hotel and were standing in the lobby discussing their recent tournament victories. After about an hour, the manager came out of the office and asked them to move. 'But why?' they asked, as they walked off. 'Because,' he said 'I can't stand chess nuts boasting in an open foyer.'

How many Oxford students does it take to change a light bulb? Two - one to change the bulb, the other to say loudly how he did it as well as any Cambridge student.

A Warboys man fell out with his in-laws and banned them from entering the house while he was in it. His wife faithfully carried out his wishes until she was on her death bed and then asked sadly, "Haven't I always been a supportive wife to you, John?" "Yes my dear." He replied "The best". "Then I would love it if you could grant my last request and let my sister Sarah ride in the first car with you at my funeral?" "Alright, my dear" he agreed heavily, "But I'm warning you, it'll spoil all my pleasure!"

A rather cocky man working on a busy construction site in Cambridge was bragging that he could outdo anyone in a feat of strength. He made a special case of making fun of Morris, one of the more senior workmen. After several minutes, Morris had had enough.

"Why don't you put your money where your mouth is?" he said. "I'll bet a week's wages that I can haul something in a wheelbarrow over to that outbuilding that you won't be able to wheel back."

"You're on, mate," the over confident young man replied. "It's a bet! Let's see what you got."

Morris reached out and grabbed the wheelbarrow by the handles. Then, nodding to the young man, he said, "All right. Get in."

I am seen in places that appear to need me not.
I come seldom to places that need me most.
Sometimes my arrival is celebrated.
at others times I am hated.
I refresh all things whether they need it or not.

Rain.

A couple from Cambridge had been courting for nearly twenty years. One day as they sat on a seat in the park, the woman plucked up the courage to ask, 'Don't you think it's time we got married?'

Her sweetheart answered,

"Yes, but who'd have us?"

Light as a feather.
Nothing in it.
Few can hold it.
For even a minute.

Your breath.

A man walked into a bookshop in Cambridge and said "I hope you don't have a book on reverse psychology."

What walks all day on its head?

A nail in a horse shoe.

The more you take, the more you leave behind. What are they?

Footsteps.

What, when you need it you throw it away, but when you don't need it you take it back?

An anchor.

What is it that you can keep after giving it to someone else?

Your word

Did you hear about the man who was convicted of stealing luggage from Cambridge Airport?

He asked for twenty other cases to be taken into account.

What jumps when it walks and sits when it stands?

A kangaroo.

A vicar from Cambridge was travelling home one evening and was greatly annoyed when a young man, much the worse for drink, came and sat next to him on the bus.

"Young man," the vicar, declared in a rather pompous tone, "Do you not realise you are on the road to perdition?"

"Oh, drat and botheration," replied the drunken man, "I could have sworn this bus went to Linton."

When is a yellow dog most likely to enter a house?

When the door is open.

What's green and runs around the garden?
A hedge.

How do you make a sausage roll?
Push it!

Two snowmen are standing in a field. One says to the other
'That's funny, I can really smell carrots.'

There are many good things to come out of Oxfordshire - most of them roads leading to Cambridgeshire.

A man enters a dark cabin. He has just one match with him. There is an oil lamp, a wood stove, and a fireplace in the cabin. What would he light first?

The match.

At a cricket match in Kimbolton, a fast bowler sent one down and it just clipped the bail.

As nobody yelled "Ow's att" the batsman picked up the bail and replaced it.

He looked at the umpire and said "Windy today isn't it?".

"Yes," said the umpire "It is. Make sure it doesn't blow your cap off when you walk back to the pavilion ".

Did you hear that they've crossed a Newfoundland and a Basset Hound? The new breed is a Newfound Asset Hound, a dog for financial advisors.

"Brothers and sisters have I none, yet that man's father is my father's son" who is "that man"?

That man is your son.

Unusual Cambridgeshire place names

Abington Pigotts

Eye

March

Prickwillow

Ramsey Forty Foot

Stow cum Quy

Wendy

Westley Waterless

How many surrealists does it take to screw in a lightbulb?
Banana.

What does one star say to another star when they meet?
Glad to meteor!

An Englishman, Irishman and a Scotsman walk into a bar.
The Barman says 'Is this a joke?'

A fresher who had just started her first term at Cambridge University asked a third year student: "Can you tell me where the library's at?"

The older student quickly said, "At Cambridge, we never end a sentence with a preposition."

The fresher had a second go: "Can you tell me where the library's at, you wally?"

What is it that never asks you any questions and yet you answer?

Your phone.

Three university friends, one each from the universities of Cambridge, Oxford and Manchester, decided to pool their funds and head to a major sporting event in Barcelona. However, because their airfares and hotel rates used up most of their money, they didn't have enough to get into the stadium to see the events.

They stood around the gate, watching all the other people get in and suddenly noticed that some people didn't have to pay. Whenever an athlete passed the guard with their equipment, the security guard would simply nod and let them through. So the three visitors quickly rushed off to a nearby hardware shop and came back to try to get in.

The Cambridge student walked up to the guard and gestured at the long pole he carried. "Pole vaulting," he said, and the guard waved him through.

The Manchester student, having rigged up a ball to a length of chain, approached the guard next and showed of his wares. "Hammer throwing," he said, and the guard shrugged and waved him through.

The Oxford student came last, with a roll of chain link on his shoulder. "Fencing."

Four retired men from Cambridgeshire were walking down a street in London. They suddenly noticed a sign that said, "Old Timers Bar - All drinks 10p." They looked at each other and then went in, feeling very excited.

The man behind the bar said, "Come on in and let me pour one for you! What'll it be, gentlemen?"

Each of the men ordered a martini. In no time the bartender served four delicious cocktails and said, "That'll be 10p each, please."

The four men stared at the bartender for a moment, then at each other. They couldn't believe their good luck. They paid the 40p, finished their drinks and ordered another round.

Again, four great cocktails were produced, with the bartender again saying, "That's 40p, please." They paid the 40p, but their curiosity finally got better of them. They'd each had two cocktails and hadn't even spent a pound yet. Finally one of them said, "How can you afford to serve cocktails as good as these for a 10p apiece?"

"I'm a retired car mechanic," the bartender said, "and I always wanted to own a bar. Last year I won the lottery and decided to open this place. Every drink costs 10p. Wine, spirits, beer - it's all the same."

"Wow! That's some story!" said one of the men.

As the four of them sipped at their cocktails, they couldn't help noticing seven other people at the end of the bar who didn't have any drinks in front of them and hadn't ordered anything the whole time they'd been there.

Nodding at the seven at the end of the bar, one of the men asked the bartender, "What's wrong with them?"

The bartender said, "They're retired people from Oxfordshire. They're waiting for Happy Hour when drinks are half-price."

Why do seagulls live by the sea?
Because if they lived by the bay they would be called bagels.

Why was the scarecrow promoted?
He was outstanding in his field!

What is the longest word in the English language?
Smiles. Because there is a mile between its first and last letters.

In the middle of an exam at Cambridge University, one student suddenly asked the invigilator to bring him cakes and beer. When the invigilator rightly challenged this, the student said "I request and require that you bring me cakes and ale!". He then produced a copy of the four hundred year old laws of the university which were still nominally in effect, and pointed to the section which read:

"Gentlemen sitting examinations may request and require cakes and ale".

The invigilator eventually produced some soft drinks and snacks and the student completed his exam whilst enjoying his refreshments. Three weeks later, the student was fined five pounds for not wearing a sword to the exam.

An Oxford University student was hitchhiking back to town at night when he got caught in the middle of a big storm.

It was growing darker and no cars seemed to be coming by. The rain was so heavy that the student could hardly see a few feet ahead of him.

Suddenly, he saw a car slowly coming towards him and stopped. Desperate for shelter and without thinking about it, he jumped into the car and closed the door. But then he realised there was nobody behind the wheel and the engine wasn't on.

The car started moving slowly. The student looked out and saw that the car was approaching a bend in the road. Terrified, he started to pray, begging for his life. Suddenly, just before the car hit the verge, a disembodied hand seemed to appear from nowhere through the car window and turn the wheel. The student stared in horror at the hand, though it didn't come near him.

Soon after, he noticed the lights of a pub appear down the road. He found the strength to leap out of the car and ran towards it. Wet and out of breath, he rushed inside and started telling everybody about the horrible experience he had just had.

A silence fell on the people in the pub when they realised how scared the student was.

Suddenly, the door opened, and two other people walked in. Like the student, they were also soaked and out of breath. Looking around, and seeing the student standing shaking at the bar, one said to the other...

"Look mate..... there's the idiot that got in the car while we were pushing it!"

What do you do if you are driving your car in central London and you see a space man?
Park in it, of course.

Two aerials meet on a roof - fall in love - get married. The ceremony was rubbish - but the reception was brilliant.

Why couldn't Cinderella be a good soccer player?
She lost her shoe, she ran away from the ball, and her coach was a pumpkin.

Three men were using the urinals in a public lavatory. The first man did what he needed to do, zipped up, walked to the sink and thoroughly washed his hands, using plenty of soap and water. As he was drying his hands with lots of paper towels, he announced:

"At Oxford University, I learned to be clean and sanitary." The man then left the bathroom looking very pleased with himself.

The second man zipped up, went to the sinks, and cleaned his hands with far less soap and water than the first man, though still being very thorough. As he was drying his hands (with one paper towel only), he announced:

"At LSE, I learned to be clean and sanitary, but I ALSO learned to be thrifty and environmentally conscious."

He then strode out of the bathroom very proudly.

The third man finished, zipped up, and sauntered past the sinks to the door, muttering to himself:

"At Cambridge, we were taught not to wee on our hands."

Six dozen dozen is greater than half a dozen dozen   yes or no?

No, both are equal.

In your first year at Oxford, you learn more and more about less and less, until you know everything about nothing.

In your final year, you learn less and less about more and more, until you know nothing about everything.

Your mother's brother's only brother-in-law is your Stepfather, Grandfather, Uncle or Father?

Your Father.

Language student to teacher, 'Are 'trousers' singular or plural?'
Teacher, 'They're singular on top and plural on the bottom.'

Why was the computer so tired when it got home?
Because it had a hard drive!

What do you get when you cross a dog with a telephone?
A Golden Receiver!

What do cats like to eat for breakfast?
Mice Krispies

What kind of ears does an engine have?
Engineers

What do you get if you cross a nun and a chicken?
A pecking order!

Four Oxford University students taking chemistry at university had done very well in their exams so far.

Because of this, even though their last exam of the year was fast approaching, the four friends decided to go back to their home town and catch up with some friends there.

They had a great time. However, after all the fun, they slept all day on Sunday and didn't make it back to town until early Monday morning which was the morning of their final exam.

Rather than taking the exam then, they decided to find their professor afterwards and explain to him why they missed it.

They told him that they had gone home to do some study for the weekend with the plan to come back in time for the exam.

But unfortunately, they had a flat tyre on the way back, didn't have a spare, and couldn't get help for a long time. As a result, they had only just arrived now!

The professor thought it over and then agreed they could make up their final exam the following day.

The four were very relieved. They studied hard that night - all night - and went in the next day at the time the professor had told them.

He placed them in separate rooms and handed each of them a test booklet and told them to begin. The first problem was worth five points. It was something simple about a specific chemistry topic.

"Great," they all thought, "This is going to be easy."

They each finished the problem and turned the page.

On the second page was written, 'Question 2 (for 95 points): Which tyre?'

John, an Oxford graduate was disappointed to hear that his application to gain a postgraduate qualification at Cambridge University had been rejected.

It turned out that putting "Because it's God's plan" as the answer to every question on the application form wasn't the best way to get in.

What always ends everything?

The letter 'g'.

What lies at the bottom of the ocean and twitches?

A nervous wreck.

What's the difference between roast beef and pea soup?

Anyone can roast beef.

How many Oxford dons does it take to change a light bulb?
Change!? What do you mean CHANGE!?!?

A group of backpackers from Cambridge University were sitting around a campfire one dark evening when a stranger asked to join them. Glad to add to their group, they agreed. The evening's fun soon turned to jokes. One of the students started to tell jokes in which Oxford was the butt of the humour. The stranger who, it turned out, had graduated from an Oxford University himself, became more and more furious with each quip. Finally, he had had enough and pulled out his razor and began to threaten the group with it. Fortunately for them, he couldn't find an socket to plug it into.

A man went on a trip on Friday, stayed for two days and returned on Friday. How is that possible?

Friday is a horse!

Three friends, from Cambridge, Loughborough and Oxford universities respectively, were out having a good time together at a funfair. They were just about to go on the helter-skelter when an old woman stepped in front of them.

"This is a magic ride," she said. "You will land in whatever you shout out on the way down."

"I'm up for this," said the Cambridge student and slid down the helter-skelter shouting "GOLD!" at the top of his voice. Sure enough, when he hit the bottom he found himself surrounded by thousands of pounds worth of gold coins.

The Loughborough student went next and shouted "SILVER!" at the top of his voice. At the bottom he landed in more silver coinage than he could carry.

The Oxford student went last and, launching himself from the top of the slide shouted "WEEEEEEE!".

A man walks into a doctor's office with two onions under his arms, a potato in his ear and a carrot up his nose. He asks the doctor: 'What's wrong with me?'

The doctor replies: 'You're not eating properly.'

What time does Sean Connery arrive at Wimbledon?
Tennish.

A well known Philosophy professor from Oxford was giving a lecture on the philosophy of language at Cambridge University and came to a curious aspect of the English language. "You will note," said the somewhat stuffy scholar, "That in the English language, two negatives can mean a positive, but it is never the case that two positives can mean a negative." To which someone in the back responded, "Yeah, yeah."

What five letter word can have its last four letters removed and still sound the same?

QUEUE - remove "UEUE", say Q. Q and queue are pronounced the same.

A man from Cambridge called Tom was having a pint at The Eagle one night when Bob, a loud mouthed chap from Oxford, walked in. Tom couldn't help overhearing Bob trying to encourage some people to bet that they couldn't drink 20 pints in 20 minutes. Despite a great deal of persuasion, he was still failing in his attempt to make some money. Bob then looked at Tom and said "Well what about you then? Are you interested?" Tom quickly drank the rest of his pint and left the pub.

Half an hour later, Tom walked back the pub and said to Bob "OK, I'll take that bet."

Bob was delighted at the thought of winning the bet. But his excitement soon faded when Tom drank down the 20 pints in 19 minutes. Handing over the money, Bob said "When you left here earlier, where did you go?". Tom looked at him and replied "I had to go to the pub down the road to see if I could do it first."

One afternoon at Oxford University, a group of freshers who had just started their Psychology degree were attending one of their first seminars. The topic was emotional extremes.

"Let's begin by discussing some contrasts," said the tutor. He asked one student "What is the opposite of joy?" The student thought about it briefly, then answered "Sadness," The tutor then asked of another student "What is the opposite of depression?" . She paused then said "Elation,"

"And you," the tutor said to another student sitting in the front row, "What about the opposite of woe?". The young student replied, "Um, I believe that would be 'giddy up".

A man from Oxford was weaving his way home, after a heavy night at the pub with his friends.

He suddenly noticed a man from the water board with a big 'T' handle, in the middle of the road opening a valve at the bottom of a manhole.
He walked up behind him and gave him a shove.

"What was that for?" asked the startled man.

The drunk man replied, "That's for turning all the streets round when I'm trying to find my way home!"

At the Varsity match one year, a big group of Oxford supporters, unable to get tickets, stood outside the stadium shouting up at Cambridge supporters for updates on the state of play. Suddenly there was a massive roar from the crowd, so the Oxford supporters outside shouted up, "What's happening? What's happening?". The Cambridge supporters shouted back, "All the Oxford team have been carried off injured. There's only one player left on the field". Ten minutes passed. Then there was another massive roar from the crowd. The Oxford supporters shouted up "What's happening? Our player scored, has he?".

A lawyer from Oxford and a businessman from Cambridge ended up sitting next to each other on a flight to Cambridge Airport.

The lawyer started thinking that he could have some fun at his fellow passenger's expense and asked him if he'd like to play a fun game. The Cambridge man was tired and just wanted to relax. He politely declined the offer and tried to sleep. The lawyer persisted, explaining:

"I ask you a question, and if you don't know the answer, you pay me only £5; you ask me one, and if I don't know the answer, I pay you £500."

This got the Cambridge man a little more interested and he finally agreed to play the game.

The lawyer asked the first question "What's the distance from the Earth to the moon?"

The Cambridge man said nothing, but reached into his pocket, pulled out a five-pound note, and handed it to the lawyer.

Now it was the Cambridge man's turn. He asked the lawyer, "What goes up a hill with three legs, and comes down with four?".

The lawyer used his laptop. He used the air-phone, he searched the web, he sent emails to his most well read friends, but still came up with nothing. After over an hour of searching, he finally gave up.

He woke up the man from Cambridge and handed him £500. The man smugly pocketed the £500 and went straight back to sleep.

The lawyer went crazy not knowing the answer. He woke the man up and asked, "Well! What goes up a hill with three legs and comes down with four?"

The man from Cambridge reached into his pocket, handed the lawyer £5 and went back to sleep.

I am so small, and sometimes I'm missed.
I get misplaced, misused, and help you when you list.
People usually pause when they see me,
So can you tell me what I could be?

A comma.